D1603886

What the Victorians *Didn't* Do for Us

A collection of their useless advice

Beatrice Hemsworth

summersdale

WHAT THE VICTORIANS DIDN'T DO FOR US

Copyright © Summersdale Publishers Ltd, 2005
Additional text by Rebecca Hughes and Charlotte Bincham

Condition of Sale

Summersdale Publishers Ltd
46 West Street
Chichester
West Sussex
PO19 1RP
UK

www.summersdale.com

Printed and bound in Great Britain

ISBN 1 84024 468 2

Contents

Introduction

Nobody can deny that the Victorians did a lot for us. But they occasionally blundered in the midst of all the industrial advances and incredible discoveries. History has largely overlooked these errors in judgement and relegated them to their grubby place firmly under the carpet. We've gathered together these dusty facts so that you can appreciate the enormous diversity of Victorian society, from their habit of clinging to bizarre medical practices to their preposterous – and sometimes deadly – beliefs.

Queen Victoria reigned in Britain from 1837 to 1901 and passed many misguided beliefs onto her subjects. Her reign was not a smooth one, however. She survived seven assassination attempts, three of which took place in 1842. Nevertheless she managed to lead her subjects in a merry, albeit remarkably strange, dance of morality, innovation and contradictions. Some of the revelations within this book will make you smile, some will make you cringe; but we believe that all should be remembered.

Values in Society

All Hail the Queen!

Despite being a woman in a position of considerable power, Queen Victoria didn't have much faith in women's ability to think for themselves. When the campaign for women's suffrage began in 1865, she claimed that the thought of allowing women to vote was a 'mad, wicked folly'. She declared that feminists should be whipped and that women would 'surely perish without male protection'.

She also hated politics, a subject that became taboo among respectable Victorian ladies. At one point she announced to her daughter, Vicky: 'I am sick of all this horrid business – of politics and Europe in general, and think you will hear some day of my going with the children to live in Australia, and to think of Europe as of the moon.'

She had an unusual fear of bishops too. Her 'bishopophobia' is thought to have begun in her childhood when she developed a fear of their wigs.

Home is Where the Heart Is

The Industrial Revolution of the eighteenth and nineteenth centuries changed the face of England. Cities became huge, ugly, overpopulated metropolises where crime and disease were rampant. Machines replaced those employed in country areas and these people flooded into cities in search of work. To accommodate the new urbanites, housing was built quickly and cheaply without care for human needs: rooms were cramped and often housed entire families; indoor plumbing and clean, running water were unheard of; and very few houses had windows, never mind gardens. These slums were dirty, unhygienic places that bore little resemblance to the comfortable houses of the affluent upper classes.

In an age when individuals were encouraged to know their place, poor people were advised to fill their beds with beech-tree leaves, which 'smelled grateful' and wouldn't contain vermin. As a bonus, the leaves made the beds very springy.

From Rags to More Rags

The population increased dramatically during the Victorian era but this meant that thousands suffered under the burden of poverty. The typical Victorian attitude was to ignore the affected masses in the hope that they would somehow disappear. The upper classes, in particular, had no sympathy for the poverty-stricken and claimed that most people were poor because they wasted their money on alcohol and gambling.

———⟫●⟪———

Mrs Cecil Francis Alexander included this verse in her uplifting hymn 'Maker of Heaven and Earth' (better known as 'All Things Bright and Beautiful':

The rich man in his castle,
The poor man at his gate,
God made them, high or lowly,
And ordered their estate.

This verse is usually omitted today but summed up the Victorian disposition perfectly. They firmly believed that each person had their place in life and wouldn't have dreamed of interfering with God's plan. It's not surprising that this point of view was upheld more by the comfortable upper classes than the starving lower classes.

Elegant Elocution

Only the Queen's English was acceptable, and speaking in a regional dialect or a different accent was frowned upon. Those with different – or, as the Victorians saw it, wrong – accents were pitied and encouraged to change their intonation for a more appropriate one. One expert on the English language, Mrs Mortimer – author of *The Clumsiest People in Europe* – noted that the Scottish accent was very broad:

> *One day a traveller said to a Scotchman, 'Does it always rain, as it does now?'*

> *'No,' replied the man, 'it snaws sometimes.'*

> *He said 'snaws', instead of 'snows', for the poor Scotch speak their words very broad.*

An English City Garden

The Victorian era was one of increasing levels of pollution and sprawling city slums as a result of the Industrial Revolution and the fast expanding population. However, it also witnessed a growing interest in the more eye-pleasing hobby of gardening, and during the nineteenth century local governments created myriad city parks and municipal gardens. Yet their efforts were less an attempt to spruce up the suburbs and more a bid to crack down on antisocial behaviour; these green areas, it was said, would encourage a peaceful disposition and discourage drunkenness, especially among the poor.

Educating Victorians

While education has always been a subject for debate, the Victorians' main worry was not about raising educational standards. Instead, many expressed their concerns about the very idea of educating poor, working-class children, as it was feared that teaching them to read and write would lead them to disagree with their 'elders and betters'.

Life for those who were educated was not always a bed of roses, however. Those children who didn't behave exactly as they should suffered cruel and unusual punishments devised by the powers-that-be. The following are just a few examples:

The log – Unruly students were forced to sit with a log strapped to their shoulders.

Pillory and stocks – Children's heads and wrists were strapped into the holes of the wooden plank or pillory while their ankles were bound in the stocks. Naturally this was quite an ordeal for the child, causing considerable discomfort and and fear.

The cage – Very naughty children were placed in a basket which was then hung from the ceiling. Victorian schoolteachers no doubt took their cue from the gibbet, a device used to display criminals' bodies and deter other wrongdoers.

As a messenger boy or errand girl, a child could expect to earn as much as three or four shillings a week; but only if their nails were in good condition.

Childish Industry

Child labour took on many delightful forms in Victorian England. In most working-class families, children were expected to contribute to the family's income, and, due to their age and lack of education or experience, the children had to take on rather menial jobs. These included positions in mining – crawling through tunnels too narrow for an adult to fit through; and in factories – scrabbling under lethal machinery in order to fetch stray cotton bobbins. The smaller the child, the more jobs they could do.

———————

Many a young child worked as a chimney sweep, with employers using them in place of brushes. The children were simply dropped head first down the chimney and were expected to clear up any blockages they encountered along the way with nothing but their hands. This commonly-used method caused substantial damage to quite a number of craniums, hence the phrase 'daft as a brush'. If the exhausted child ever fell asleep or became wedged in the chimney, their master would light the fire beneath them to make them work harder.

Bringing up Baby

After the Bastardy Law was passed in 1834, all children born out of wedlock were declared the sole responsibility of the mother, absolving the father of any duty towards his offspring. These children were never given the opportunity to support their families, however. Instead, they were sent to 'baby farmers' – those involved in the child extermination business – to make sure that the mother's shame wouldn't impact on her future, and wouldn't interfere with her employability.

What's in a Name?

Added to the difficulties of being a child in the Victorian era was the psychological damage caused by the popular names of the time. Abishag, Lettuce, Water, Tram, Clapham, Despair, Murder, Ham, Feather and Brained were just some of the monikers parents chose for their beloved little ones.

It was not advised to wake a child with a sudden noise, or to carry them from a dark room into glaring light as this was believed to damage infant eyes.

Diagnosis: Madness

In the Victorian era, any illness that didn't appear to have a physical cause or cure was treated under the blanket diagnosis of madness. Asylums, which started as charitable hospitals and institutions for those afflicted with illness, became places of horror where people were confined indefinitely and often for little reason. Amendments to the Poor Law meant that councils could use the asylums to rid themselves of the undesirable elements of society, both the genuinely unstable and the poor, thus making poverty a crime in England.

———◆———

The word 'lunatic' stems from a Latin word and describes a type of madness provoked by the movements of the moon, which may explain why so many women suffering from PMS were committed as madwomen.

It was believed that, although all women could succumb to hysteria, the most susceptible were spinsters, whose unfulfilled uterus would cause them considerable anxiety. Yet, paradoxically, medical discourse defined a woman as one who bore children; therefore a spinster was not a woman at all.

Mad Dogs and Englishmen

The Eighth Earl of Bridgewater was an interesting fellow and had a typical Victorian outlook on life. He was not, however, the most orthodox person. One of his favourite hobbies was the popular sport of pigeon shooting. When he grew older and his eyesight was no longer what it had been, he ordered his servants to trim the wings of the pigeons so they would slow down and he would have a better chance of hitting one of them.

Furthermore, he had little leather boots made for his dogs in order to protect their paws, and dined with them every evening. They wore white napkins at the table and he indulged in what was presumably a rather one-sided conversation whilst they ate.

I Believe...

Those living in the Victorian era were fearful of anyone with a different racial or class background to their own, while any kind of physical deformity and women's sexual powers were the stuff of Victorian nightmares.

These are some everyday Victorian superstitions, some of which have spilled over into modern life, despite having no basis in reality:

Planting yellow flowers in the garden would protect your family from the looming threat of witches.

———❧❧❧———

If a lady had a spare silver coin, she should place it under her pillow on Valentine's eve to attract a proposal by the end of the year.

———❧❧❧———

New shoes were never placed on the table as this was thought to cause the wearer's death within a year.

Good luck could be achieved by wearing an item of clothing inside out. It could also be encouraged by placing old shoes in the rafters of the house.

————⇒●⇐————

A leek in the attic protected a house from fire.

leak   roof

————⇒●⇐————

On Shrove Tuesday, people made sure to throw the first pancake they made to their hens, to guarantee plenty of eggs for the remainder of the year.

————⇒●⇐————

Those with a bit of a cash-flow problem were advised to turn over the coins in their pockets, preferably while staring at the moon. Another way to bring those pennies in was to wash your floor.

Death Becomes Them

We all like to treasure mementoes of our loved ones. In order to keep the memory of the deceased alive, Victorians developed the habit of photographing their dead. However, it involved more than just a simple snapshot – they liked to dress their dearly departed mother, father, son or daughter in their Sunday best and pose them in lifelike positions for one last family portrait. These photos of the dead were a common feature of Victorian houses. ⟶ Really?

A Time of Mourning

The mourning customs adopted by Victorians spoke more of their adherence to social niceties than true grief. A person in mourning was expected to follow strict guidelines, which included an acceptable length of time to grieve your passed loved one. Those who failed to follow the mourning rules risked being sent to social Coventry.

———⟫●⟪———

Mourning was divided into two parts: deep mourning and half mourning. Mourning a spouse meant a year of deep mourning followed by a year of half mourning. Deaths of other family members were also mourned but for different lengths of time. A sibling was to be mourned with three months of deep mourning and three months of half mourning while the loss of a parent or a child necessitated nine months of deep mourning and three months of half mourning.

———⟫●⟪———

Women were required to wear dresses of sombre black crape during periods of deep mourning but were allowed to change into silk dresses for the length of the half-mourning period, as long as the dresses were black. Only specific jewellery could be worn – black cut glass, jet, amethysts and pearls – and then only during this second part of the mourning process. Some women followed Queen Victoria's lead and wore black for the remainder of their lives.

The tradition of wearing a black veil during mourning came about because Victorians believed that the soul of the departed person would cling to those to whom they were close during their life. The veil acted as a shield that prevented this ghostly attachment. Mirrors were covered to prevent the dead person's soul from becoming trapped in the reflective glass.

A Family Show

It was legal to hang people publicly until 1868. Many people thought this was an excellent spectators' sport and often brought the whole family to the event. The struggle of the condemned person and the potential for blood and gore, as well as the gossip surrounding the crime and execution, appealed to the Victorian sense of the macabre.

It was advised to carry the body of a dead person out of the house feet first because if the deceased one's eye focused on the house, it would call others to death.

A Dog's Death

Victorians had a penchant for drama and held elaborate funerals – for the family pet. They included specially-written poems and hymns in the ceremony and then laid their beloved Dash or Little Miss Puss to eternal rest in the pets' graveyard; an area frequently found in public parks and the gardens of stately homes.

———⟫●⟪———

Other 'civilised' Victorians who struggled with the idea of not seeing their beloved pets again, had them preserved, and gave them a rather morbid place of honour in their homes. It is likely that visitors often mistook these motionless animals for extremely well-behaved pets.

Fashionably Dead

Using poison to kill someone became known as the 'fashionable' crime: it was an easy and clean way of dispatching someone to an early grave and was popular with those who were eager to get away with murder. Poison wasn't easily traced because forensic science wasn't very advanced, and police could never prove that the deceased hadn't died of natural causes. The development of the life insurance industry undoubtedly contributed to this trend, as it became all the more tempting for the greedy few to poison a wealthy family member and claim the life insurance bounty for themselves.

———⇒●⇐———

Many women killers used the chemical arsenic, although strychnine was also favoured. Arsenic was readily available since it was often used around the home as a form of rat killer and could also be found in some women's cosmetic bags.

Social Graces

Battle of the Sexes

Aside from Queen Victoria's personal opinion that women would simply fade away without a man to take control, the belief that a woman's place was in the home had biological beginnings. It was thought that because men only concerned themselves with the act of fertilisation, they had the time and energy to follow other pursuits. Women, on the other hand, were preoccupied with menstruation and had rather a more active role in procreation. It was, therefore, considered logical to teach young girls how to sew and manage a household instead of more intellectual activities.

Nice Girls Don't Do That

Sex was not a popular topic of conversation among respectable Victorians. They believed that if a man reached sexual climax, it would have a direct negative effect on his physical strength, even to the point of bringing him closer to death. Just as importantly, his moral resolve would be lessened. But it was also believed that a man couldn't be held responsible for his urges and, because women weren't affected quite as badly by the power of sex to deplete the human body, it was a wife's responsibility to ensure that she and her husband only engaged in marital relations to procreate. Of course no nice Victorian girl would dream of doing more than kiss her prospective husband before getting a ring on her finger.

———❧———

This distaste for sex also affected the way people thought, as Victorians were sure that just thinking about the deed would eventually lead to insanity. Anyone who was tempted by sexual desires was firmly encouraged to repress those thoughts and concentrate on less devilish sentiments. Those who could not control their naughty impulses lived lives of secret shame while awaiting their final damnation.

Women suffered a loss of vitality during sex but, because they could withstand the deprivation, it was a common practice for many young girls and women from the lower classes to work as prostitutes to pay the bills. Men could visit prostitutes and not be harmed socially but the women were forever 'fallen' and had no hope of ever recovering a decent position in society.

———————

Homosexuality was strictly illegal in Victorian England and given the typical Victorian attitude towards sex in general, it is not surprising that Oscar Wilde, writer, husband and father, was convicted because of his so-called 'homosexual offences'. He was relatively lucky to be sentenced to two years' hard labour because for the majority of the nineteenth century, homosexuality was punishable by death. The last execution on these grounds took place in 1830.

Just Say No

The Reverend Thomas Malthus was certainly a man of this very prudish time. The Victorians were concerned that there would come a time when they would be unable to feed all the hungry mouths of the expanding population. 'Malthusianism' advocated marrying late in life and having as little sex as possible as a valid, though partial, solution.

That Time of the Month

One of the many taboos in Victorian times concerned menstruation. Although it was understood that menstruation was necessary, it was also believed that mental excitement could bring on a woman's monthly flow suddenly and upset her health. It was up to the men in women's lives to control the frequency of their menses by, as far as possible, keeping the female members of the household calm and quiet. Women, therefore, were seen to have no control over their monthly physical condition and were pushed into the role of weak, subservient female.

———————

Women were advised to use the following remedies to ease the pain of menstruation:

Cupping the loins
Placing the feet in warm water
Avoiding hot rooms
Sleeping less
Avoiding any kind of mental excitement

There wasn't a lot of medical literature available for Victorian women and the little that existed was written by men who, with a vague idea of how menstruation really affected a woman's body, dubbed it a female disease and relegated it to the area of domestic medicine. Some doctors even believed that if the menstrual flow was blocked, the blood would be forced to the woman's brain, causing irreparable harm.

⟶⟫●⟪⟵

Doctors postulated that menstruation caused such physical strain that young girls were incapable of dealing with the intellectual demand of schoolwork as well. It was widely believed that girls exceeded boys in all aspects of life until the age of puberty when they became disabled by menstruation. During menstruation, the girl would discard huge amounts of 'pelvic power', allowing boys to overtake her in every way. Indeed, it was thought that if a woman tried to learn mathematics, her brain would overheat.

The only way literacy during the Victorian era could be measured was by counting the signatures on the marriage register. In 1850, although 69% of men could sign their names, only 55% of women could manage this. This was due to the fact that only middle- and upper-class girls were taught to write. Apparently there wasn't any need to teach the girls of a lower social order to even sign their own names.

Being Miss Right

It is a well-known fact that etiquette for young ladies was extremely rigid in Victorian times. If they failed to comply with the rules as set out by society, their chances of making a successful marriage could be destroyed. But if they worked hard, they would be admired as well-brought up, dignified and graceful young ladies of good social standing, and would generally be considered a good match.

But how did they prove their worth and bag the ideal husband?

Victorian society had many conflicting ideals for the fairer sex: despite the importance of appearing highly acceptable to others, ladies were advised not to brag or flaunt any aspect of themselves; it was never appropriate for a lady to advertise her skills at the expense of her contemporaries.

⸺⊰⊱⸺

It was considered bad taste for a young lady to show off her beautiful set of pearly whites by laughing more than necessary. But, although those who were less well-endowed in the dental area may not have felt like giggling, they had to be careful not to laugh *less* than was required in a given situation.

A young lady was advised to play the harp only if she had presentable and pretty arms. Those who failed the test took up embroidery or tapestry making instead.

———❦———

When introduced to a gentleman, a lady had to bow her head and say, 'I am happy to make your acquaintance' or another phrase of this kind, without offering her hand.

———❦———

When acknowledging another person on a public street, it was acceptable for a lady to incline her head slightly while keeping the rest of her body upright.

———❦———

A well-brought up young lady was encouraged not to take an interest in politics.

When on any form of public transport, every self-respecting lady strove as best she could to sit at a distance from her fellow passengers so as not to come into contact with strangers.

———➤●◄———

A lady was strongly advised never to stare at other people on the street or at a public venue, such as the theatre or concert hall.

———➤●◄———

Crossing the street was an adventure in propriety for the Victorian lady. She was taught to use one hand (and one hand only) to lift her dress up slightly and draw it to the right. If she used both hands to raise her dress, she ran the risk of exposing too much ankle, which was considered highly indecent.

Tinkling the Ivories

For many women, playing the piano was a favourite pastime and an acceptable party piece. But one journalist in 1871 noted that practising scales also provided ladies with an emotional outlet: 'A good play of the piano has not infrequently taken the place of a good cry upstairs; and this was important [in a society that] frequently calls upon her to repress her feelings.'

Social Sergeants

The chaperone was an important part of Victorian society. They maintained control over their charges, preventing the possibility of impropriety and scandal, and also ensured that young people weren't swept into the horror of marrying beneath them. Young, unmarried ladies were not allowed to walk alone and could never ride in a closed carriage with a man who was not a relative. They were expected to be in the company of a chaperone at all times – an older, married lady or a male member of a lady's family were considered suitable. If a lady (married or not) called on an unmarried man at his home or entertained a gentleman in her home without having a suitable chaperone present, then chaos would ensue and she would lose her respectable place in society.

Some Victorians believed that when a man reached eighty five years old, he was still a man, but once a woman passed forty, she was no longer regarded a woman.

The Art of Calling

Calling on social acquaintances was severely regulated with more 'don'ts' in the list of advice than 'do's':

Don't call on a lady before 2 p.m. or after 4 p.m.

Don't leave your hat in the hallway. Bring it with you to allay your host's fears that you intend to remain for more than just a short visit.

Do send your letter of introduction ahead of making a personal visit.

Don't bring a small child or a dog with you.

Don't usurp your host's duties. Allow them to perform introductions and instruct their servants as they wish.

———⇒❦⇐———

Don't move your host's furniture or possessions, don't open the window or touch the curtains unless you want to appear meddlesome and interfering.

———⇒❦⇐———

Don't include topics such as politics, religion or gossip in your conversation.

Meeting and Greeting

Mutual friends were a social necessity in Victorian times as they determined how those of different social standing could meet and also how young people were introduced to their future spouses. This ensured that only personages of suitable social rank ever had contact and decreased the chances of making an inappropriate match.

───≫●≪───

It also meant that having friends in relatively high places was absolutely essential if you wanted to find a friend in a very high place indeed, as a person of lower rank could never approach a person of higher rank without a formal introduction, and then only if that exalted person was agreeable to the idea.

───≫●≪───

Unfortunately for those trying to climb the social ladder, the higher ranked person was never obliged to maintain contact after the introduction.

Flirting with Fans

Fans were an extension of a Victorian lady's body, and were used in a language that required men to pay very close attention to every wave and flicker of the paper device. It saved courting couples the bother involved in actually speaking to one another, while bypassing the chaperoned conversation rule. However, if all the flirts and all the beaux knew the meaning behind the movements, it can't have been very secret, and with a limited range of movements, it wasn't very subtle either.

The movements were translated as follows:

* Fast fan movements – I am independent
* Slow fan movements – I am engaged
* Fanning with the right hand in front of the face – Leave me alone
* Fan opening and closing – Kiss me
* Fan wide open – Love
* Fan half open – Friendship
* A shut fan – Hate
* Swinging the fan – Will you see me home?
* Drawing the fan across the forehead – We are being watched
* Letting the fan rest on the right cheek – Yes
* Letting the fan rest on the left cheek – No

If a lady was not very adept at the art of fan-waving, yet the gentleman knew the meaning of every movement, it could be very easy for her to give him the wrong impression.

Say it with Flowers

This repressed society was not kind to romantic aspirations. Banned from openly communicating with members of the opposite sex, Victorian Don Juans were forced to find other means to express their emotions. Unfortunately, their use of flowers as code was just as limiting and unimaginative as communicating with fans: everybody knew the meaning of each flower and each colour, making a bouquet from a lover less of a secret and more of an indiscretion. There were even several flower dictionaries written, to help them decode the *true* meaning of their horticultural allies, although not all agreed on the same meaning of each bloom. Relationships could end before even beginning if two lovers used different dictionaries.

———➤●◄———

The idea behind floral codes originated in Turkey but in true Victorian style, the meanings expressed were diluted, emphasising courtly value instead of carnal desire.

The shade of the flower was the key to its message. A red flower, as it is still widely believed today, symbolised love; however, a white flower evoked the cryptic message 'I am worthy of you'. Mixing several flowers in one bouquet could constitute an entire conversation, albeit a confused and one-sided one.

Courting Couples

Amorous young men were not permitted to approach the young lady of their dreams without a formal introduction by a mutual friend. After this proper meeting, the man, if he wished, could offer to escort the lady home, although he could never do anything as coarse as to say the words aloud. Instead, he offered her his card.

———◦———

Before the evening drew to a close, the lady would look at all the cards she had acquired (because, as everybody knows, it's best to keep your options open) to decide upon the most suitable young man to accompany her. Once she had come to her final decision, she would contact the gentleman by giving him her card, indicating that he was the lucky winner.

They were then permitted to converse and to be seen together in public in the presence of a chaperone. While out walking, the couple could not make physical contact although the gentleman could offer his arm to assist the lady in walking over rough patches.

———◦◦◦◦———

Sexual activity of any nature was forbidden until the wedding night and it was the lady's responsibility to ensure that intimate contact never took place. After all, a young lady was seen as good and proper only as long as her chastity and innocence were intact, whereas men were constantly preoccupied with sex and couldn't be held accountable for their natures.

———◦◦◦◦———

Once the young man was satisfied that circumstances were developing favourably, and neither of them had been exchanging cards with other suitors, he could ask the lady for her hand in marriage. After the lady had agreed to his proposal, he was then expected to ask permission from her parents.

After 'I do'

A couple's married life was also controlled by social traditions. Wives were strongly advised not to pester their husbands, especially when something in particular may have been bothering him. Instead, they were encouraged to wait until he felt the time was right to share his troubles. They were also taught to treat their men like superior beings and to act suitably awed by their wisdom.

———◦———

Those who wanted to spend more time with their husbands, or who just wanted to avoid spending a boring evening staring at the back of his newspaper, were taught to read the newspaper before their husband arrived home and relate the stories to him over dinner.

———◦———

Once married, a woman ceased to legally exist as an individual, and her body and material possessions were owned by her husband. In fact, it wasn't until 1891 that a judge ruled that it was no longer acceptable behaviour for a man to imprison his wife. Up to that point a husband could do what he wished with his wife and could even beat her with a stick if he was so inclined. However, it was stipulated that the stick could not be wider than his thumb.

Some women embraced becoming one with their new spouse and even took their husbands' titles as part of their new name. And so young women dreamed of being Mrs Captain Scott, or Mrs Dr Baker or even, Mrs Col Robinson. Of course, it didn't hurt that this habit advertised their husbands' importance, and by extension, their own.

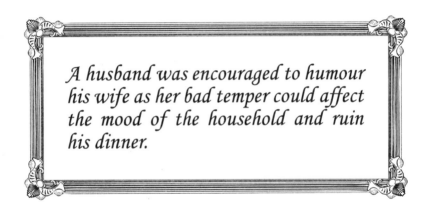

A husband was encouraged to humour his wife as her bad temper could affect the mood of the household and ruin his dinner.

Keeping Up Appearances

Looks Are Everything

The Victorians' fascination with people's physical appearance may have stemmed from their obsession with silent communication. But whatever the origin, they truly believed that the science of phrenology – looking at people's faces and figures – gave a valuable insight into the inner workings of their minds.

Even Charlotte Brontë subscribed to this belief. In Chapter 14 of *Jane Eyre*, first published in 1847, Jane examines Mr Rochester, whose brow 'showed a solid enough mass of intellectual organs, but an abrupt deficiency where the suave sign of benevolence should have risen'.

Victorians admired the robust appearance of their monarch, Queen Victoria. Yet, the weak and frail beauty was also appreciated: 'languishing', 'expiring', 'fainting', 'fading' were words used to describe desirable qualities in a lady. To get the best of both worlds, most ladies looked after their health but drank vinegar when they wished to appear delicate and dainty.

To lengthen the eyelashes, it was advised to cut the ends with a pair of scissors once a month. Mothers often cut the eyelashes of their infant sons and daughters to create the desired effect.

Socially Correct Couples

It was crucial that a couple *looked* like a couple and, while a man and a woman were courting, they individually assessed their possible future spouse for compatible aesthetic characteristics. There were rules and guidelines put in place for those who weren't sure what they were hoping to see:

Two people with the same eye colour should never marry.

Someone who possessed wiry features and cold blood was advised to search for a partner with rounded features and warm blood.

It was a widely-accepted fact that people with bright red hair had an excitable temper, therefore, the partner they chose needed to balance them out; someone with dark hair was recommended.

Any person with soft fine hair was advised to attempt to find someone with an entirely different hair type.

A curly-haired person was a perfect match for a person with straight hair.

Crowning Glory

Hair type was a clear indication of a number of different character traits. It was widely believed that it had links with both class and sexuality.

———✦———

Light-coloured hair was seen as proof of a full-blooded and generous temperament. Victorians believed that blondes with white skin and blue eyes were kind and tender.

———✦———

Dark hair had darker connotations, and was connected with a '*bilious* habit of body, a muscular and nervous temperament, a dark and yellowish skin, lively black eyes, and a bold, proud air'.

The Crime Race

Victorians didn't limit their knowledge of phrenology to finding the perfect partner; they also used it to fight crime. They believed the crime gene was passed on through generations and showed itself in facial characteristics. If the eye was trained carefully, it was possible to spot one of these creatures from afar, enabling the more cowardly members of society to run away quickly. Unfortunately for any innocents with these features, the Victorians didn't believe in their own fallibility.

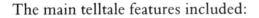

The main telltale features included:

* Boils

* A low forehead

* Warts

* Heavy, dark eyebrows (there were clearly no blonde thieves)

* Close-set eyes

* Defined bumps on the forehead

* A pointed chin

* A dirty face

Teething Pains

Cleaning your teeth in Victorian times didn't involve minty-fresh goodness as much as it did salty flavour. Salt was recommended as the ideal toothpaste because of its gritty, abrasive qualities. Then, to achieve the ultimate dazzling smile, it was advised to use charcoal as a whitener.

———⟫●⟪———

Before the invention of fillings, toothaches were dealt with in an uncomplicated manner – the offending tooth was simply pulled out. But there were few anaesthetics available to be administered, so the patient had to grin and bear the pain as best they could. Perhaps that's where our fear of dentists originated?

———⟫●⟪———

You could, however, have false teeth. They were made of carved ivory, wood, animal's teeth or, if you were lucky (and rich), poor people's teeth – selling their teeth was one way the poverty-stricken masses could make some quick cash. It may have been preferable not to have any teeth at all because these replacements rotted quickly, becoming oddly coloured and smelly.

Fashionably Painful

Victorian women had a very strict wardrobe and wore as many as twelve items at any one time. Their underwear alone weighed almost fourteen pounds and could never be seen by anybody except close family relatives, a doctor or a personal maid.

———◆———

No self-respecting lady would leave her house without each of these items:

* Stockings

* Drawers

* Chemise

* Corset

* Petticoat – often more than one

* Crinoline

* Underskirt

* Overskirt

* Gown – which could be a full dress or consist of a separate skirt and bodice

* Shoes

* Accessories – such as jewellery, gloves and a fan

* Hat or bonnet

Ladies spent hours getting dressed, a task which was virtually impossible without the aid of at least one other woman. Some ladies even had to change several times a day as certain dresses were only suitable for particular occasions and no lady would go to dinner in the same dress she had been wearing while taking her daily constitutional.

And Breathe In...

Corsets are a classic example of Victorian clothing. But, despite how hugely fashionable they were, they were extremely uncomfortable. Unfortunately for those who disliked feeling restricted, any lady who left the house without her corset was considered 'loose' (and this did not refer to her physical state).

Some ladies found it extremely difficult to breathe while wearing corsets and many fainted. This habit reinforced the belief that women had a fragile nature and needed to be protected, preferably in the home.

The solution to this predilection for swooning was not for the faint-hearted, however. Those ladies who were eager to be out and about simply had a rib removed.

Corsets were stiffened with whalebone and around fifteen thousand whales were killed each year to support fashion-conscious Victorian ladies.

The Importance of Being Regular

Training to wear a corset began at an early age when the novice fashionista was encouraged to achieve one bowel movement early each morning before slipping into her outfit for the day. This prevented the inconvenience of having to remove the elaborate layers of underwear in order to do one's business later in the evening. Some ladies took this to an extreme and injected an enema to assist in the daily ritual. They even took it so far as to pack their very own enema equipment for those trips away from home.

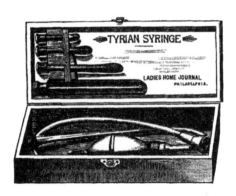

On Top of the World

Another classic example of top-class Victorian fashion, the top hat, was not always favourably received. John Hetherington proudly donned his creation and walked the streets of London. Women fainted, children screamed, dogs yelped and one unfortunate errand boy had his arm broken when he was trampled by the mob of terrified onlookers. The bewildered Hetherington was promptly taken to court for wearing 'a tall structure having a shining lustre calculated to frighten timid people'.

Fancy a Nightcap?

'The Crimean Nightcap' was the dream accessory for every keen traveller. All you needed was a handkerchief and the ability to fold:

* Take one large, clean handkerchief.

* Unfold the handkerchief into its natural square form.

* Turn down one third.

* Lift it up and turn it over, so that the third folded down is under the rest of the material.

* Place it over your head and tie it beneath your chin.

Milliners must have feared for their livelihoods.

Going for a Dip

In an age of morality and modesty, men and women who did not wish to draw attention to themselves when going for a swim in the sea, used the 'bathing machine'. This popular contraption enabled seabathing without being so crass as to expose your flesh. These machines were large wooden devices with a roof and walls that could be used as a changing cubicle and then rolled into the sea so the bather could enter the water without showing more than their heads and arms.

Domestic
Functions

A Private Inconvenience

Before indoor plumbing became commonplace, people made do with chamber pots, which were stored under the bed and emptied by the maid, or they trudged outside to the little huts at the bottom of the garden.

Several inventors claim to have created the first flushing toilet but it's widely acknowledged that the company of Thomas Twyford of England invented the first all ceramic toilet in the 1870s. Twyford's developed their skills by making teapots.

Victorian gentlemen prided themselves on their excellent aim and made use of an unusual ally in the public water closets. Above each urinal was a picture of a bee. The aim of the game was to hit the bee. Although this seems a strange choice, the fact that the Latin word for bee is *apis* perhaps answers some questions.

Cleaning products for carpets included tea leaves or fresh cut grass. Grass was highly recommended as tea leaves sometimes left stains on the carpet, while the grass left a bright and fresh appearance.

Food, Glorious Food

While thousands starved, the royal family had the pick of the best food available. Prince Edward, Queen Victoria's eldest son, favoured hot turtle soup for his morning snack. This was after his usual breakfast of milk, eggs, bacon, toast with butter, fish and chicken. After dining on a twelve-course meal, he had the habit of bringing a cold roast chicken to bed in case he felt a little peckish during the night.

━━━━━━━━━◦━━━━━━━━━

In order to stretch their limited food sources, mothers were advised to teach their children to chew very carefully and slowly as this would ensure that they would require much less food.

━━━━━━━━━◦━━━━━━━━━

A root plant in Indonesia bears a striking resemblance to a small lamb. The discovery of this 'lamb vegetable' thrilled Victorians who believed they had finally found the connection between animal and vegetable.

Here is a small collection of the era's culinary highlights:

Bread Jam

* Cut the crust from five slices of stale bread and toast the slices until they are lightly browned.
* Place them in four pints of boiling water and add a few slices of lemon.
* Let this boil into a jam and then, let it cool down fully.
* Strain it and sweeten for taste.
* If you don't particularly like lemon-flavoured jam, then you could use wine and sugar to spice the bread instead.

Mushroom Ketchup

* Cut up a quantity of large mushrooms and cover them fully in salt, and then leave them for two nights. Then, strain the liquid out of the mushrooms and add it to a pan with black pepper, sliced ginger, shallots and horseradish.
* Boil these ingredients for several minutes and then strain the mixture.
* Once it has cooled, decant into bottles, taking care to cover the bottles very tightly.
* The ketchup should keep for up to three years.

Sheep's Head

* Cut open the head and remove the whole brain in one piece.
* Remove the tongue and place it in cold water. Take care to wash the brain and the tongue well.
* Divide the head in two, taking out the eyes, cutting the gristle from inside the nose and shortening the jaw-bones where there is no flesh.
* Rinse the head well in clean water.
* Put the two halves of the head and the tongue into a large pot of cold water and add some salt. When the water comes to the boil, add the brain, two large onions and three large carrots, and leave to boil for a further fifteen minutes.
* Serve the head on a dish with the onions and carrots laid round them. Alternatively, mash the onions into a sauce, adding salt, pepper, butter and milk to taste.
* Cut the tongue in half and pour some of the broth over the top.
* Heat the brain in the broth, then place it in a dish and sprinkle sage powder and some of the broth over it.
* Add rice or oatmeal to the broth to make a wonderfully tasty soup.

To Work or Not to Work

There were not many career options for Victorian women. Those of a lower class were consigned to work in factories or to find positions as maids while upper-class women were expected to run their husbands' households. They tended to act in more of a supervisory position and rarely, if ever, got their hands dirty, instead employing an army of maids to cook, clean and launder His Lordship's socks. Any sewing that the high-born lady of the house undertook was purely decorative.

———◆———

A maid was expected to work an average of sixteen hours a day, from six in the morning until ten at night. This allowed her to take care of details such as lighting fires and preparing breakfast before the mistress awoke, while ensuring that she would be present for additional chores until the moment the lady of the house fell asleep. While maids were often young girls, older women with families and households of their own often worked as cooks or maids to supplement their family's income.

One industry that employed women was the matchmaking industry. This wasn't a dating agency or a network of anxious mothers eager to marry off their daughters. Instead, women were forced to work long, hard hours for minuscule wages, wages that would be reduced if the worker in question was caught gossiping on the job or was even one minute late for her shift. They were also susceptible to several diseases, including phosphorus necrosis, also known as 'phossy jaw'. It was caused by the white phosphorus used in the manufacture of the matches and caused the sufferer's teeth and jaw to swell and produced a pungent and unpleasant pus, as abscesses formed in the jawbone. The only potential cure was to remove the rotting jawbone, leaving the patient completely disfigured.

The phrase 'mad as a hatter' does not come from Lewis Carrol's *Alice's Adventures in Wonderland* but from the symptoms experienced by those working in millinery. Mercury was used to turn fur into felt and workers were constantly exposed to the metal's poisonous fumes in the badly-ventilated workshops. Symptoms included vehement shaking, forgetfulness, persistent clumsiness, irritability, slurred speech and anxiety. Some unfortunates even lost their teeth.

On the Road

The motor car was a wonderful invention. It opened up broad new vistas and gave people the opportunity to explore more than just the land outside their front doors. But it also gave us pollution, traffic congestion and a disturbingly high number of road-related deaths.

In 1896, the speed limit increased by an amazing 400%, from a measly 4mph to a staggering 20mph. Was it the beginning of speeding as we know it today?

Twenty-five-year-old taxi driver, George Smith, damaged the reputation of taxi drivers everywhere when he became the first (but, unfortunately, not the last) drunk driver. On 10 September 1897, after drinking several glasses of beer, he drove his taxi onto the footpath and crashed into 165 Bond Street in London.

The first ever road death occurred on 23 September 1897 when nine-year-old Stephen Kempton was crushed by a London taxi.

The Hard Stuff

Since beverages of the intoxicating variety were much easier to get hold of than decent drinking water, drunkenness was a distinct problem in Victorian times, even amongst the very youngest members of society. A mother's handbook advises feeding two-year-old children a 'light and well-fermented table beer' in the event that water wasn't available. This may well have been a contributing factor to the statistic in 1842 that half of all children died before they reached the grand old age of five.

It wasn't until 1872 that Victorians realised that getting their children drunk was not the best way to raise their offspring. In this year, alcohol retailers were prohibited from selling spirits to anyone under the age of sixteen. In 1886 this ban was extended to beer, but alas, only for people under thirteen years of age.

———⟫●⟪———

The higher classes condemned the excessive use of alcohol, claiming that nasty things would happen to those who had too many tipples. It was considered highly likely that any offspring the adult drinker managed to produce would either be insane, an idiot, an invalid or suffer from hysteria.

Playtime

Popular sports of the time had themes of death and destruction, and were considered an appropriate manner of expressing dangerous tendencies:

Football was a much more dangerous game in Victorian times than it is now; there were few rules and lots of subsequent bumps, bruises and broken bones. Even after rules were brought in to ensure everybody had jolly good fun (and to make sure that nobody could call in sick to work), the play was more foul than fair. Free kicks and penalty kicks were introduced to penalise the players who liked shin kicks. Women were even allowed to play but spectators at one match played in Glasgow in 1892 were horrified by the unladylike behaviour of the players, calling it 'the most degrading spectacle we have ever witnessed in connection with football'.

One sport that was very popular amongst working-class women was boxing. These vicious, bare-knuckle fights often ended with competitors suffering serious injuries. Some fighters were celebrated for their ability to beat up other women, such as 'Bruising Peg' and 'the famous boxing woman of Billingsgate'.

———◆———

Pigeon shooting reached the height of its popularity in the 1880s and it was considered a great skill to shoot pigeons accurately and in great numbers. Clay pigeons were invented in the 1880s to prevent the real ones becoming extinct. Shooting pigeons was a valid way of increasing your social standing and many men vied eagerly for the elusive invitations to shooting parties at the great estates of the rich and famous.

Gardeners of a respectable dwelling first buried a dead donkey before planting a grapevine.

Let Me Entertain You

The development of the steam engine allowed shows in Victorian England to expand and develop more elaborate rides and attractions. Road-run locomotives meant that showmen could discard the slow horse-drawn carriages and pile enormous weights onto trailers. Unfortunately, construction of the road network wasn't developing quite as fast and often the roads collapsed beneath the weight of the trailers.

Freak shows were the mainstay of entertainment because Victorians loved the macabre. They loved looking at the albinos, fat men, two-headed women and living skeletons. They especially enjoyed the Elephant Man, getting a vicarious thrill from gawping at these unfortunate creatures. They never considered the human element behind the bizarre figures and treated the freaks like performing animals. Perhaps entertainment like this was the inspiration for today's *Big Brother* and various other reality TV shows.

Foreign Affairs

Britannia, Britannia

One fifth of the world was part of the British Empire during the Victorian era. The British reaped the benefits by pouring the natural resources of their colonies into the imperial coffers. They laid claim to diamonds from South Africa, cotton from Egypt, tea from India, slaves from Africa and the Caribbean and to sweeten it all off, sugar from the West Indies.

The Charge of the Light Brigade

On 25 October, 1854, 637 men charged Russian soldiers in what Benjamin Disraeli described as a 'feat of chivalry, fiery with consummate courage, and bright with flashing courage'.

⟫●⟪

But no matter what the Victorians claim, the Charge of the Light Brigade was not a brave attempt to rout the enemy and claim glory for Britain. It was a case of mistaken identity and misunderstood orders. The leaders of the brigades were high-born but not particularly competent: Lord Lucan ordered his men to charge the enemy without being sure of his true target while Lord Raglan failed to take into account that those in the valley did not have the advantage of his elevated position.

⟫●⟪

This is one of the most famous incidents from the Crimean War, despite the fact that it resulted in only 157 deaths out of a total of 20,000 killed during the entire war.

It's Not the Winning, it's the Taking Part That Counts

The shortest war in the world was fought between the mighty forces of the British Battle Fleet and the spice island of Zanzibar. The Sultan's second son, Said Khalid, took the throne after his father's death in 1896 with the blessing of the German occupiers. But the British couldn't accept this turn of events because they didn't want the Germans to take control of the island. At 9 a.m. Khalid was ordered to leave the palace. He dug his heels in and refused.

———>•<———

At 9.02 a.m., fighting broke out and at 9.45 a.m. the war ended when the British fleet used a mere two shells to sink the only battleship owned by Zanzibar.

Out of Sight, Out of Mind

In another example of the Victorian tendency to ignore the things they couldn't be bothered to change, convicts were sent to Australia on the other side of the world. Nicknamed 'getting the boat', this practice meant that more than 150,000 British people of all ages and genders were shipped 'down under' with no thought of rehabilitation or of how the thousands of criminals would survive once they reached their destination.

———➤●◄———

Many died on the way but those that made it through the voyage were forced to eke out a life in a new land with no hope of returning home. As well as ridding England of an unsavoury element, these convicts were used as cheap labour in the initial colonisation of Australia.

Not all the criminals were rapists and murderers, some had simply fallen foul of the new economy and couldn't pay their debts. Some were sent away for stealing a loaf of bread.

———➤●◄———

While the guilty few were waiting to be brought to their new homes, they were held on board ships, called 'hulks', that were moored in the Thames. These hulks were initially used as temporary living quarters but remained in place for much longer, housing petty criminals in later years.

Travel Tips

Victorian travel advice was certainly unique but in most cases, recovering from illness on a journey was due to luck rather than sage advice.

————⟫●⟪————

The best cure for an upset tummy was a pinch of gunpowder in a glass of warm soapy water.

————⟫●⟪————

It was best to remove your clothes to save spoiling them if you were caught in a tropical storm. Clearly, modesty was not as important as a smart jacket.

————⟫●⟪————

Soaking your socks in soapy water was the best protection for blisters, as long as you put the socks on before they dried and cracked an egg into each boot before setting off on your day's trek.

It was advised to treat savages with a forthright, humorous and positive manner. It was also advised to pretend to have more confidence in their good faith than you might feel. For the many Victorians who felt that anyone who wasn't British was a savage, this was general rather than specific advice.

Wearing a well-ventilated hat guarded against the possibility of one's head overheating.

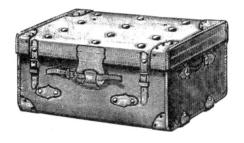

Superiority of the Whitest

The Victorians' lack of tact and understanding of the various social classes in their own country extended to their relations with other races. British imperialist Cecil Rhodes, that master of racial diplomacy, said:

'First look for the race that God has chosen to be the Divine instrument of future evolution. Unquestionably that is the white race. Whites have clearly come out top... in the struggle for existence and achieved the highest standard of human perfection... Therefore I shall devote the rest of my life to God's purpose, and help Him to make the world English.'

We all know what a good idea *that* was.

The Irish Question

Some scientists of the age declared that it was possible to see which race was inferior by examining the structure of the jaw and skull. They deduced that, as well as being Celts, the Irish had an ape-like structure of face and, therefore, were quite low down in the hierarchy of Victorian society. This ape-like theory caused consternation among (superior) Anglo-Saxons.

———>●<———

In 1860, historian Charles Kingsley visited Ireland and wrote to his wife concerning the people he saw whilst he was there, many of whom were still struggling to recover from the crippling Irish Potato Famine:

I am haunted by the human chimpanzees I saw along that hundred miles of horrible country... to see white chimpanzees is dreadful; if they were black, one would not feel it so much, but their skins, except where tanned by exposure, are as white as ours.

The Jewish Question

During the terror created by Jack the Ripper's spree of murders, anti-Semitic feeling grew because of a questionable link between Jewish workers in the city and a possible suspect who wore a leather apron: Jews worked in professions such as butchery and tailoring, which required workers to don leather aprons. This dubious connection pushed racist and nationalist attitudes to the forefront of society and several Jewish men were attacked by scared Londoners.

The elusive Jack signed his nom de plume at the bottom of several letters to the police. Several theories about his identity were proposed, including one that claimed he was a member of the aristocracy. If the police knew anything, they certainly didn't share it and Jack the Ripper was never caught or brought to justice.

Mrs Mortimer's Worldly 'Wisdom'

Mrs Favel Lee Mortimer wrote a book in 1855 about the different countries of the world, detailing the characters of the inhabitants and the various customs of each place. Strangely, Mrs Mortimer made only two trips outside England in her lifetime and developed her oft-repeated advice purely on rumour and hearsay. Here is a minute selection from the wealth of her remarkably offensive, and yet typically Victorian, opinions:

> Is London a pretty city? No; because it is not built at the seaside or on high hills.

> Though the Welsh are not very clean, they make their cottages look clean by white-washing them every year, and sometimes they white-wash the pig-sties too.

> You would not like the sound of the Scotch bagpipes. The noise is almost as ugly as the creaking of a door, or the squalling of cats.

The poor Irish men are fond of drinking and keeping company with friends; but they often quarrel with them, and then they call them names and throw things at them, and cover them with bruises.

———◆———

French parents keep children up late, and let them eat unwholesome food.

———◆———

Very few Spanish people like reading or any useful employment.

———◆———

Coachmen in Russia are sent to Siberia if they run over a person in the streets. This makes them very careful, but it makes the people very troublesome. Instead of getting out of the way, they will look up at the coachman, and say, 'Mind Siberia.'

In Italy there are plenty of stalls in the towns where macaroni is sold, and the poor people in the evening go and buy their supper, and you may see them holding up this serpent-like food and letting it slip down their throats.

Yet though the Russians are generally not to be trusted, I have heard of one who acted in a very upright manner.

———➤●◄———

No people in Europe are as clumsy and awkward with their hands as the Portuguese. It is curious to see how badly the carpenters make boxes, and the smiths make keys.

In Norway after service the Sabbath is not kept holy. There is dancing, and drinking, and merry making. No wonder therefore that most people are very ignorant.

Turks are so grave that they look wise. But how can lazy people be really wise? They like to spend their time in eating opium, sipping coffee, and sitting still.

Greeks do not bear their troubles well; when they are unhappy, they scream like babies.

The Chinese are proud of their country, and think there is none like it. They look upon foreigners as monkey and devils.

It is very wicked for a man to kill himself, yet in Japan it is the custom for all courtiers who have offended the emperor, to cut open their own bodies with a sword. The little boys of five years old, begin to learn the dreadful art. They do not really cut themselves, but they are shown *how* to do it, that when they are men, they may be able to kill themselves in an elegant manner. How dreadful!

———⟫●⟪———

The worst quality in any character is hypocrisy, and this is to be found in the Egyptian.

———⟫●⟪———

South Africans used to drink to excess, and they do so still; they used to delight in idleness, and they used to tell lies, and they do so still.

The World of Science

The Earth

Victorians firmly believed that our planet was shrinking. Their logic dictated that as the Earth cooled, it contracted and took on the wrinkly characteristics of a prune.

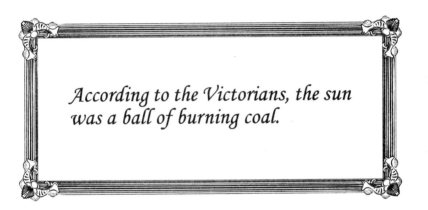

According to the Victorians, the sun was a ball of burning coal.

Dinosaurs

William Buckland was the first to realise that the very large, fossilised bones he discovered near Oxford belonged to lizards of an enormous size but it was in 1842 that Richard Owen coined the phrase 'dinosaur', meaning 'terrible lizard'. Victorians were awfully excited and dinosaur fever spread rapidly across the nation. Even Prince Albert claimed to be a fan.

―――――>●<―――――

Richard Owen had several life-size models made from his drawings of the beasts yet they weren't entirely accurate. He didn't find all the bones of each creature, so he used his imagination to fill in the missing pieces. He instructed Benjamin Hawkins, the sculptor responsible for making the dinosaurs for the Sydenham Park exhibit, to make the creatures look more like mammals despite the lizard connection.

Other scientists put together their own dinosaur models but following in Owen's footsteps, they used a rather unusual structure. One scientist put a dinosaur together completely back to front, placing its head on the end of its tail and proudly photographing his creation. One of his more observant contemporaries informed his rival of his error, provoking much embarrassment on the wronged scientist's part.

Origin of Species

Charles Darwin first put forth his concept of the origin of species in 1859 but it wasn't accepted until the twentieth century. Victorians were not keen on the idea that they evolved from apes because it didn't suit their belief in their paramount importance in the world. However, it did fit in with their feeling that people are born either poor or rich and nothing should be done to change the situation.

First Attempts

Robert Cocking has the dubious privilege of being the first man to die in a parachuting accident. In 1837 he designed an inverted cone-shaped parachute and jumped from a height of 5,000 feet. The parachute worked well for the first few minutes but then descended too rapidly for comfort.

———⟫●⟪———

In 1875 Matthew Webb became the first man to swim the English Channel, triumphantly navigating the currents without the help of artificial devices. High on his success, and eager to win the £12,000 prize, he decided to brave the currents of Niagara Falls eight years later. After only ten minutes, he was swept under the water and died in the attempt.

———⟫●⟪———

Percy Pilcher wanted to be the first man to fly an airplane. He tested his theories on flight with hang gliders but refused to 'free fly', preferring to be towed along instead. It was certainly a safer method of flying but cannot have helped to advance his ideas. He plummeted to his death in 1899, without ever flying a powered aircraft.

Live Operations

Before the invention of the television, people had to look elsewhere for entertainment. Advances in science and medicine allowed those with a liking for the macabre to witness scientific experiments, autopsies and even live operations. True fans always chose to sit at the front of auditoriums, because the first few rows were warned, 'You will get wet.'

Let There Be Light

While gas lights were a wonderful invention, the light produced wasn't very strong and they were also prone to exploding. They also covered the lamp in soot, which eventually made its way around the room, and indeed the entire house. Many people made do with candlelight and oil lamps and it wasn't until the Houses of Parliament converted to gas light that Victorians jumped on the fashionable bandwagon. Electric lights weren't much better; invented in 1809, they did not last long and since they consisted of two wires joined to a piece of coal, they didn't quite light up the whole house.

Chemical Maze

In 1862, the Privy Council estimated that a fifth of butchers' meat wasn't fit for human consumption – some animals had even died from diseases before the meat was sold to the public. Ten years later Dr Arthur Hassall made some disturbing discoveries about the actual ingredients of food:

Strychnine was found in rum and beer.

———➤●◄———

Sulphate of iron was one of the ingredients in both beer and tea. Chinese tea had a large amount of ferric ferrocyanide and lime sulphate among its leaves.

———➤●◄———

Pickles, wine, jam and bottled fruit contained sulphate of copper.

———➤●◄———

Lead chromate was detected in snuff and mustard.

Copper carbonate, lead sulphate, bisulphate of mercury and Venetian lead was found in sugar confectionery and chocolate.

———➤●◄———

Wine and cider contained lead.

———➤●◄———

It took a long time for people to realise that staple foodstuffs such as milk, butter, bread (and gin) contained more unappetising, stomach-ache-inducing chemicals:

* milk was found to contain far too much water and strangely, too much chalk;

* a high percentage of butter, bread and gin contained copper which had been added to heighten the foods' colour;

* and Gloucester cheese got its distinctive colour from the excessive quantities of red lead.

The Recorded Word

After the invention of the phonograph, demonstrations were met with scenes of public hysteria. People claimed that hearing their voices played back to them was the result of black magic. Others dismissed the invention, regarding it as a hoax.

The Magic of Electricity

English inventor, Dr George Scott, was very excited by the discovery of electricity but was rather too enthusiastic in its application. He was a prolific advertiser in America in the 1880s with unusual items such as electric plasters and electric body belts. Other inventions included:

* Electric insoles

* Electric rheumatic rings

* Electric anklets

* Electric shoulder braces

* Electric throat protectors

* Electric nerve and lung invigorators

* Electric wristlets

* Electric leg appliances

Dr Scott claimed that his electric hairbrush could cure several illnesses including diarrhoea, asthma and bronchitis. Apparently it also provided ease from spinal complaints, lameness and even paralysis.

Curious Cures

And You're Feeling Sleepy...

One treatment that was used in the early part of the Victorian era was hypnosis. Doctors used this as an anaesthetic and believed that they could operate on a patient in a hypnotic trance with few side effects. Admittedly it had some advantages – it caused no pain and it did not affect heart rate. However, very few people could be hypnotised into a deep enough sleep to withstand long operations and many people weren't affected by hypnosis at all.

—————➤●⊂—————

John Elliotson, a popular practitioner of phrenology, was converted to mesmerism in the 1830s and is responsible for the widespread appeal of the theory in Victorian England. Named after the Austrian doctor, Franz Anton Mesmer, this treatment was formed around the idea that human bodies were infused with a fluid that was the basis of physiological processes and could be affected by magnets. Mesmer believed that the movements of the planets could disturb this fluid by means of gravity, causing illnesses and even breakdowns. He taught his followers that some people had the power to heal others by simply staring into their eyes or touching them.

Despite the popularity of both hypnosis and mesmerism, the fear that practitioners would take advantage of unconscious patients led Victorians to abandon these remedies. However, they did not abandon other medical practices that were used regularly and were just as strange.

Making the Pain Go Away

One of the strangest procedures used by Victorian doctors was phlebotomy or bleeding. The idea was to cleanse the body of the 'bad blood' causing the illness. Doctors cut the patient with a lancet or used leeches to suck the blood out. This weakened the patient further, making it more difficult for them to fight their initial affliction.

———➤●◄———

Victorians used bread and milk, and at times, cow manure, to create a sticky paste that was then plastered over cuts, scrapes or bruises. It was also used to treat internal diseases such as pneumonia.

———➤●◄———

Purging was a very popular cure. It constituted feeding the patient laxative substances, in order to rid the body of 'poisons', through the actions of both diarrhoea and vomiting.

Doctors advised bundling sick people up in warm blankets to sweat the illness out of them. They also recommended plunging the patient into a bath of cold water and keeping all fresh air out of the sick room.

———➤●◀———

Victorians firmly believed that only one illness could affect a person at any one time, so they scoured patients' skin with hot pokers or acid to force the sickness out.

———➤●◀———

In an era where symptoms and not causes were treated, amputation was the most frequently performed medical operation. If a doctor couldn't cure an illness, he simply cut off the offending limb. Due to the rather casual attitude towards sterilisation, more often than not it was surgery that caused the patient's death.

Smoking

In 1851, the first ever cigarettes were sold in Britain and were praised as a miracle cure for illnesses. Unfortunately for those well-to-do young ladies who felt a bit queasy, smoking was severely frowned upon and any respectable lady caught with a cigarette in hand lost her boyfriend to smug, non-smokers. The need for a nicotine fix was well understood and those who wanted to light up while out for a spot of riding were advised to use their horses as shields from strong winds.

Birth Control

Victorians believed that birth control should not be used under any circumstances. They also believed that no matter what measures a woman took to terminate the life of her unborn child, she would be unsuccessful and the result would be an idiot child.

⎯⎯⎯➤●◄⎯⎯⎯

Taking feng shui to a whole new level Victorians agreed that if the marital bed was aligned from north to south, the children who resulted from any bedtime activities would turn out to be deformed hermaphrodites.

The Solitary Vice

One belief, which admittedly some still subscribe to today, was that masturbation was the underlying cause of blindness and insanity. Victorians, however, were certain that it also would cause the male member to shrink and waste away, eventually resulting in the complete deterioration of the offending man's entire nervous system.

———◆———

If women partook in such a practice, their faces would lose colour, their hands would feel soft and clammy, their eyes would become dull and their feet would omit an intolerable odour. They could also suffer from epilepsy, insanity and premature death.

Mysterious Microbes

The Victorians weren't aware of the existence of germs, despite having microscopes available. They disagreed with one scientist who, in 1854, discovered the bacteria *Vibrio cholerae* that caused cholera. Felippo Pacini died destitute, never knowing that his theories were actually correct. Many Victorians believed that dirt could be healthy and would protect against potential illnesses. When a surgeon performed an operation, he would frequently opt to wear his dirtiest and oldest garments, rather than spoil his cleaner (and less infected) clothes.

———⇒●⇐———

It wasn't until the mid-1860s that Londoners ceased to rely solely on water pumped in from the River Thames. Before this, they used water to cook and clean, despite the fact that it was consistently added to by the contents of over two hundred sewers.

Feeling Good

Opium was popular in the medical profession for a number of reasons, one of which was that its effects were 'immediate, direct, and obvious' and according to Dr Jonathon Pereira because 'its operation is not attended with pain or discomfort'. The main advantage of opium, however, was the lack of short-term side-effects. Unfortunately for those for whom it was frequently prescribed, this magic drug was highly addictive. Doctors were well aware of this fact, yet they overlooked this minor hiccup and failed to alert their patients.

Laudanum was a popular drug among Victorian insomniacs. A mixture of both opium and alcohol, this liquid was frequently taken as a sleeping medicine. It also worked as a painkiller, a way of preventing loose bowels and as a cough-suppressant. However, the laudanum-happy Victorians were unaware that they were addicted to the dream medicine and took doses in their dozens. Not wanting to appear greedy (and to avoid being disturbed by their little ones) they also used the mixture as a quick and easy way to quiet babies.

Homegrown Cures

The Victorians invented a staggering array of remedies for just about every complaint a person could have, the vast majority of which could be concocted easily at home. Unfortunately most 'cures' had no effect whatsoever.

———❧———

Victorians entertained the idea that the inability to sleep was caused by blood pressing on the brain. Insomniacs were seen as over-excited individuals, often of a nervous disposition. They advocated brushing the body to promote circulation as this deliberate chafing calmed the brain and allowed the sufferer to get a relaxing night's sleep.

They mixed caraway seeds with ginger and salt and spread the mixture over buttered bread. It was believed that eating this rather strange sandwich twice a day would calm the nerves.

The cure for rheumatism was a sticky concoction of goose grease, horseradish juice, mustard and turpentine, to be liberally applied to the area of complaint.

Apple juice was used to destroy warts. Rubbing half an apple on the offending protrusion was thought to cause the wart to fall off a few days later. They also believed that drinking elderberry juice would cure facial warts.

Holding the feet of a dead chicken against your body aparently cured ague (a violent fever with added chills).

The father of a child suffering from whooping cough was told to bring the child to a field at sunset and gently hold their head in a hole.

Cow dung was an approved remedy for burns, although those living in more urban areas had to search hard for this substance and swore by a simple covering of wheat-flour instead.

Parents hung the foot of a dead mole around their baby's neck to ease the pain of teething.

The perfect cure for a nosebleed was to place a nettle leaf on the tongue and press it up against the roof of the mouth. If a nettle leaf was not available, then the best course of action was to place a large key against the skin of the back.

Rubbing an onion on your head was considered a cure for baldness.

www.summersdale.com